# Hope Without A Plan Is Failure

## A Guide To Live Your Best Life

Maxwell Sears, MA, LPC

**Hope Without A Plan Is Failure**

A Guide To Live Your Best Life

ISBN: 978-1-7375007-0-4

Copyright © 2021 Maxwell Sears, MA, LPC
All rights reserved.

Published by
CAYA Counseling Services, Inc.
Stockbridge, GA

Book Design by
Williams DocuPrep
www.williamsdocuprep.com

All rights reserved. This book or parts thereof may not be reproduced in any form, stored in a retrieval system, or transmitted in any form by any means— electronic, mechanical, photocopy, recording, or otherwise—without prior written permission of the publisher, except as provided by United States of America copyright law.

Hope Without A Plan Is Failure

# Dedication

*I dedicate this book to my father and mother. To my father, who did not know the value of his child, and to my mother, who protected that value.*

# Contents

Dedication ............................................................. i

Contents .............................................................. ii

Acknowledgements ............................................. iv

CHAPTER 1

This Is My Story .................................................. 1

CHAPTER 2

Success Leaves No Evidence .......................... 24

CHAPTER 3

Failure Is A New Beginning ............................ 34

CHAPTER 4

G in Greatness is for YOU ............................... 43

CHAPTER 5

Hope Without A Plan Is Failure ..................... 53

CHAPTER 6

A Man Without A Manual Is A Mule ............. 63

## CHAPTER 7

Who Changed Your Story From Glory? .......... 71

## CHAPTER 8

What You Are Willing To Die For? ................. 92

## CHAPTER 9

Conclusion ......................................................... 101

About The Author ............................................107

Maxwell Sears, MA, LPC

# **Acknowledgements**

I want to thank God, who is Jesus Christ, the head of my life, in whom I live, move, and have my very being. I want to thank my wife Karlene for her dedication. I want to thank my siblings, children, friends, associates, ministers, pastors, legal team, and clients who have kept me accountable through this journey. Finally, I want to thank my publisher and editor Ms. Angeline Williams of Williams DocuPrep who saw the best in me to bring the truth to light in this guide.

## CHAPTER 1

# This Is My Story

*Leave the world a little better than it was because you came into it.*

I was born in the Bahamas on February 12th, 1963. At the age of eighteen, I migrated to the United States on a student visa, attended Hunter College in New York, and earned a Bachelor of Science degree in Psychology.

> *Love is not an emotion or feeling, it is an act of the will.*

Ever since then, I have been helping people alleviate themselves from the prison of their minds. I am the founder of CAYA Counseling Services, Inc., where the focus is on the greatness in all of us. CAYA means come as you are!

I often tell people that my life started with a struggle. I was born prematurely, and I am told that the labor was difficult for both of us. The first lesson I teach others is that life is full of struggles.

We all must keep moving to stay afloat! You must keep moving to stay afloat, and you must keep striving until your last breath. Life is often defined by ongoing struggles. Your first breath is a struggle, and your last breath ends the struggle. When you stop striving, you die.

My mother was a single parent who raised 12 children. She was a strong mother who taught us how to survive and conquer the challenges of life. Ironically, she could only save us from her own struggles. We all have our own battles to fight. The most vicious battles we fight are the battles within us.

My mom was looking for love. What she got were a few romantic relationships, which resulted in giving birth to twelve children. She never discriminated against any of us, but she treated all her children equally. There was never any inequality or discrimination in my mother's house. Differences are no excuse for inequality. I learned about treating people equally from my mom.

Despite the purity of her heart, my mom failed to find true love. She was seeking something outside that was inside her all that time. What she did not seek in herself, she wanted to find from someone else (which is technically impossible).

We often love the idea of love more than actually loving someone. No human being really knows what love is, so how can we expect someone to love us, if they never knew what love is. If we do not know what love is, how can we love ourselves? When we cannot find love within ourselves, how can we expect it from others?

Usually if we love ourselves for thirty percent, and the other person loves us for fifty percent, we will consider it good enough. This then becomes mentally destructive.

Mental destructiveness is living without being loved, or not being able to receive love because of the triggers caused by the traumas in our lives. A trigger is an acknowledgement that we have suffered from past pain. That is only part of the equation of why we stay loveless.

Love is not an emotion or feeling; it is an act of the will. We have an Advocate who has shown us how to love and left us a mandate to love. We must look to Him to teach us love.

Being born on an island comes with its fair share of struggles and difficulties, especially in a single parent household. Growing up on an island is vastly different from growing up in the city. Sometimes we were deprived of our basic needs, and the many luxuries others may consider a necessity. I did not know I was poor until I witnessed people who did not seem to value life.

After observing them, I realized that people often take life for granted. This is especially true when they do not have to work for what they get. You do not know the value of something if you did not strive for it; you take things for granted! We often learn to value what is taken from us.

The struggle is part of what makes life worth living. Depravity can give you a sense of responsibility. When you know you are on your own, and no one owes you anything, you become a responsible human. The struggles of life help you to mature. What others may consider a disadvantage, I learned to perceive as a chance to grow emotionally and spiritually.

Living in the Bahamas for 18 years with a single parent who had 12 children to raise is a setback that I did not ask for. I came to realize that the struggles I faced were unsolicited, nor was I at fault.

It was tempting to blame my failures on my circumstances, but instead I stood firm and used my adversity as an opportunity. Yet, in my early teens, I was not mature enough to understand and to use what was inside of me.

During my former years, I was not aware of my true worth, and the purpose of my existence. Just being born in the Bahamas and growing up in Freeport, I adopted the spirit of the island beauty. This allowed me to counter the many struggles that I faced.

Not everyone is privileged to be born or to live in the heart of nature. Given their beauty and simplicity, islands are considered the purest forms of land. When you have this awareness, you have a covering around you that saves you from the terrible things going on around you.

You are empowered not to fall into the world's trap of trying to get something for nothing, which ultimately saves you.

As I grew up on the island of Grand Baama, the beauty that surrounded me got inside. The depth, awareness, and habit of waiting and understanding what was happening, and why it was happening empowered me.

Growing up as a disadvantaged youth, I had to compete for resources, love, and opportunities, so I anxiously took advantage to explore my potential at every opportunity.

I struggled as an underprivileged student. Yet, there was a luminous presence, an awareness that was guiding me on the right path, not letting me stray from the right path, which kept me from alcohol, drugs, and crimes.

Although I grew up in a bad atmosphere, it did not have a negative effect on me because something greater than my environment was inside me. Keeping a firm spirit prevented my circumstances from engulfing or infecting me. What infects you will affect you.

Like everyone else, I have faced challenging times, but I stood headstrong in the face of adversity. I never fell for the charms of the world because it only leads to harm. I believe in the power of choice and how it drives our decisions, because choice limits excuses.

When you have awareness, you are guided spiritually. The spiritual gifts God has given me give me the light that I need, and great understanding. Eighteen formative years in the Bahamas prepared me for something beyond life, a higher purpose that I was not aware of at that time.

Maturity does not come with age; maturity comes with accepting responsibility. There are immature people out there in their forties and fifties who have never seen adversity as a responsibility. Adversity makes you a responsible human because responsibility has two key elements: choices and consequences. I call them the two C's.

In my early teens, I did not know what I was doing. Without a father figure in my life, I lacked the guidance that I needed. My difficulties were not impossibilities however, it gave me a firm foundation. With a solid foundation, no power in the universe can shatter your spirit.

I grew to empathize with others, who disliked unfairness, poverty, and inequality. The emotional bondage that keeps us in pain. My love of self-awareness brought me through the biggest tragedy in my life.

After spending 18 years on the island, I came from the Bahamas with a foundation that no one can shake. At first, I did not want to, but since I had no plans, my older brother, Alfred, convinced me to move to New York for higher studies. He helped me apply for college.

> *External solutions can never solve internal problems.*

I did not know what I should study, so for a while, I just went through the motions. I was only in the United States by chance. I got into college by chance. Sometimes, things happen by chance. You have the power within you to transform chances into opportunities.

My brother Wellington was one of a kind. Wellington was mentally challenged because of being traumatized by our grandmother. He had a hard time choosing between our mother and our grandmother on various issues. Our grandmother's cruelty towards our mother affected Wellington's mental health.

Whenever our grandmother became angry with him, she would send him back to our mother, which caused a break in his psyche. This is the reason that Wellington was diagnosed as schizophrenic and bipolar for a long while.

Unfortunately, no one understood what was actually wrong with him because the medical community only saw his affect and not his infection of being neglected and emotionally abused.

One day, as I was mending a pair of pants, Wellington was triggered and began to behave very rashly. A trigger is an unresolved childhood trauma or experiences that we bring into our adult decisions. He grabbed a pair of scissors sitting nearby on the bed, and with all his might, without care of life or what it would have done to me, and he plunged it into my chest, missing my lung by two inches and my heart by one inch.

Blood was everywhere, as I was rushed to the nearby clinic. The doctor was insensitive, like he did not care about my physical or emotional condition. He was insensitive to my agony, both physical and emotional.

My prime inspiration for wanting to pursue a medical profession was largely based on my negative experience with that doctor. I longed to heal others of their mental and physical agony. It was not just about the money.

Unaware of my internal bleeding, the clinician stitched or sewed my wound and sent me home. Once I discovered the internal bleeding, I was rushed to a hospital. The doctors at the hospital said that if I had been stabbed an inch upward, the scissors would have punctured my lungs, leading to instant death.

Surviving the near fatal attack was a life lesson. The opportunity for a second chance serves as a reminder not to waste precious time doing stupid things because each moment of life matters. The incident brought definition to how I perceive my life.

I became concerned about my young siblings above myself. If it were not for my life in the Bahamas and this tragedy, I would have been an entirely different person. Some of my siblings have reached their life goals, while others have not. The advantage that I have is the awareness of God that gives me spiritual insight.

The experience with Wellington and the doctor made me realize or recognize life's immeasurable worth. It was a second chance at life for me. I felt like I had been born again with fresher perspectives on life and better priorities. My experience drives my lust for life and life's actual worth.

We may take life for granted. We may not recognize the worth of our lives unless our lives are threatened. My experience with Wellington and the doctor gave me foundation during my years in the Bahamas. Though I did not realize it at the time, it made me a robust and resilient human being. I had no idea that the incident would shape my entire life.

Later on, I had another experience that shaped my life and gave it meaning. Sometimes it takes years to learn the lessons beyond certain incidents. We do not know how the experiences we encounter will influence our lives, especially going through hardships. Consequently, we sometimes complain, failing to see the bigger picture.

As Steve Jobs once said, "you always connect the dots backward." At first, things may appear senseless to us, and we may be unable to understand the reason for something happening to us good or bad. As we look backward, we get a better understanding. As we move forward, we can connect the dots backward and contemplate why something happened.

While I recovered from the stab wound, I stayed with my sister Karen. Karen's two sons enjoyed playing in their swimming pool, while I would just lie around watching. One day, both boys started to drown. I was so unprepared when I jumped in to save them that we all nearly drowned.

When I realized that I was not equipped, I pushed both the boys away from me so that we would not all drown, and then held on to the solid ground. After holding on to solid support, I saved the boys one at a time. This was another experience that had a very profound effect on me.

My nephews' lives might have ended tragically if it were not for my injury leading me to a stay at my sister's house. It also helped me see that all our lives are strangely connected. Not only that, but we are also peculiarly interconnected with a divine connection, whether we realize it or not.

If only we become slightly aware of that sacred bonding, we will not pay attention to small worldly failures and things that are not significant. We are placed on earth with a purpose that is often greater than we realize.

These two incidents had a profound impact on me. I may have grown up in the Bahamas, but I matured in the United States. These incidents continued to affect me long afterward. I did not realize their effect until I found myself in other environments.

Growing up with culturally and ethnically different people affected me in ways that I would have never imagined. Living in the United States made me realize my true capabilities. I never realized that I was so resilient and headstrong. I left the quiet, laid back life of the islands for the fast paced, cold, big city of New York.

Many people get blinded by the lights of New York and let its highs and lows affect them negatively. Some people get caught up and forget their roots, but I clung to my roots.

I did not let the highs of New York City affect me in any way. I recognized that New York did not make me, and I refused to allow it to break me or mold me. My strength and adaptability helped me overcome all the external pressures.

I have found that when people stick to their origins and do not get blinded by their temporary successes they succeed. Since I had a student visa, I earned the money to survive by working odd jobs. My first job was at ABC Carpet, and I still have a carpet piece to remind me of where I came from.

I was never tempted to do drugs and drink because of the pressures of living in New York. I have found that when you are high on life, everything else is secondary.

While drugs and cigarettes are a major distraction for international students who tend to be easily deceived, as well as domestic students, I refused to indulge. External solutions can never solve internal problems. My circumstances caused me to think differently than most others.

Materialistic pleasures do not satisfy spiritual needs. They are never enough. This is the reason some people are never satisfied. Greed left by itself never decreases, it only elevates. If only we understand that our soul's fuel is different from our bodies, then we will stop relying on materialistic satisfaction.

Our souls are fueled beyond wealth and power. Our souls receive sustenance from love and eternal happiness. Happiness and satisfaction come from within. No external factors can provide you with the satisfaction that arises from within.

At first, I struggled to support my family. This was followed by poverty. I feared I was falling into the same old pit I had grown up in. I later became a hoarder. I provided my family with material goods, but my love lacked emotion. I could not provide the love of a father because I had never experienced it myself.

In a thriving environment, both parents have the responsibility of playing an equal and integral role in child rearing. Children can be scarred for life when deprived of a parent. It can stay with them for their entire lives; it clings to them, and then it replicates in their future relationships.

That is what happened with me and my Ex. My Ex and I both lacked faith and trust because she had no faith in me, and I had no trust in her. Our relationship was dead. I could not cultivate the emotion I was never given, so I only gave my ex-wife and children mere material gains or stuff in the name of a father's love.

I got knocked down, but I got back up. That is my trade. I look at failure as a new beginning. I have vowed to never let a failure defeat me. After the relationship with my Ex failed, I started to think about what empowered my decisions. I decided that to avoid the same mistakes, some deep changes would have to occur.

I realized that I would keep attracting the same thing if I kept doing the same things. So, I began to look at my life from my childhood to adulthood. The introspection was the best part of my life. If we do not introspect on our lives, then we just let things happen and go with the flow.

Introspection leads to an epiphany. Before the epiphany, I was running from myself. We fear ourselves more than we fear anything else. If we realize our true potential, we can conquer the skies. We fear speaking to ourselves.

Words have power, and when we speak to ourselves, we blow life into our mortal minds. Read ahead and travel into your soul. Explore the depths of your being and unlock the potential within!

## CHAPTER 2

# Success Leaves No Evidence

*Life is chaos, success is arbitrary, and confidence is everything.*
— *[Brooklyn Nine-Nine (S06E04)]*

How do we see success? What is the lens through which we view success? How does the world portray success to us? What are the criteria through which we measure success? How do we perceive success? What is the precise key to success for us? These are questions everyone needs answers to, but no one knows. No one knows the precise formula to the equation of success.

Success is considered subjective. Everyone sees success through their own eyes the way they want to. No two successful people are perceived the same way. Every success is measured on a different scale. Not every successful person is famous, neither is every famous person successful.

When someone is successful, we measure their accomplishments by material gain and wealth. Success is perceived as something that can be weighed, or measured or something that could be displayed as a trophy to others.

However, contrary to popular belief, success is not material. Success comes from within.

---

*If you don't think of yourself as successful, no one can make you believe that you are.*

---

Success cannot be weighed on a scale or displayed as a trophy. Success is an internal feeling. You are not successful unless you feel that you are. No matter what the world says or thinks, if you do not think of yourself as successful, no one and no power in this universe can make you believe that you are.

Success is the drive that keeps you going. It is the feeling that helps you get out of your bed every morning. Success is the desire to get back up after falling. Success is emotional, not physical. This is the core reason success leaves no evidence. No one can tell you whether you are successful or not; you decide whether you perceive yourself as someone successful or not.

Material gains overpower our inner drive. Material gains are a consequence of our inner drive. Many are driven by material gains. People tend only to see what is visible to them. They ignore our hard work, our struggles, and the hardships we had to go through.

People only see our material gains that are driven by our internal success, and term that material achievement as success. Because material gain can be visualized, people do not see your internal drive, emotion, or desire to do something, but that emotion is what drives you to success.

Whether we achieve wealth in the form of money, or knowledge, or experience, it comes from some emotion that is led by our motives. The emotion (itself) is a success.

Imagine not getting out of bed. Imagine not having the will to wake up and repeat the same cycle that drives you most days. Imagine your life becoming mediocre. We are all subject to feel that way. Not every day is bright and sunny, where we wake up all chirpy and cheerful while looking forward to a successful day.

There are times when we do not want to go about the day. That feeling is worse than anything. It engulfs you. It robs you of the sense of purpose and meaning. Success is not letting that feeling engulfs you, looking that feeling in the eye, and keeping yourself motivated. Success is having the power to conquer that feeling.

While practice does not make us perfect, it does make improvement. Practice allows us to improve and become a better version of ourselves. Only God is perfect. Society often seeks perfection when it cannot be found outside of God.

Outside of God, there is not a single entity in this entire universe that can claim itself to be perfect. No living, breathing being can ever be perfect. So then, why are we looking for perfection?

I did not know I was successful until I met people who saw success as a material gain. Success is what you believe in, as well as what you believe to be your fate. The two are intertwined. You see success in what you seek.

When I moved to the United States, I met people who measured success materially. This made me think that I was not successful. Although I believed myself to be successful, I was unaware of the vision of success. Before moving to the United States, I did not know I was poor materially. Some people in the United

States determine success by your bank account or the size of your house.

Again, success is what you believe in. What you believe in is what comes to you. Belief is something that drives you. The world may tell you one thing, but your belief is what makes you or breaks you.

My belief comes from the firm foundation of living eighteen years in the Bahamas in a small house with eleven siblings and a single mom. Your foundation helps you to stand firm in the face of hardship. Those life changing incidents gave me confidence. They convinced me that no matter what happens, God is with me.

When I got stabbed, I was immature and did not know it. However, through the years, I have come to realize that those incidents have molded me into the person I am today. Had they not happened, had I not lived in the

Bahamas for eighteen years, I would have been a completely different person.

Your faith knits your belief, and you have the power within called greatness to accept or reject it, but you cannot change it. Faith and belief are interconnected. They go hand in hand. What you believe in becomes your faith, and your faith is what you do or work. That is why faith without work is dead.

> *What you believe in is what comes to you.*

Therefore, you have the power to choose your faith, but you cannot change it. You can change your belief by having a little or a lot, but faith is the substance of life, and the evidence is what you do to get what has already been prepared for you.

You must ask yourself some tough questions like whether you have the drive to get up after falling? Do you have the desire to wake up every morning to do the same mundane, monotonous routine? Are you willing to try for your dream job one more time? If you answer is yes, then you are successful.

If your answer is no, then you need to ask yourself why! Rewind your life and see why you do not feel the desire to work for that dream job you have always wanted. Or why do you not feel as enthusiastic and zealous about your work as you were on that first day?

Introspection is the key. Examining ourselves is something we should do often. Introspection provides us with many of the answers that we are seeking.

While introspection does not give us all the right answers, self-examination reveals to us whether we are on the right path or not. It is like a light, illuminating our path and giving us the direction, we need to advance and mature.

**CHAPTER 3**

# Failure Is A New Beginning

*"Man sees me as a failure. Man counts me as a failure; it is not a failure as long as you don't count it as one."*

We are failing our new generations by preaching to them that failure ends your life. Failure is not an ending; instead, it is a new beginning. Every day is a new day, and every day is alive with the beating of a new heart. Failure sometimes gives success the value and the worth, it deserves.

If we never failed, we would not look at success the way we do. Imagine a perfect world where every person is booming, and every person is happy. How would we value success then? How would our lives look if we did not know how life would look otherwise? If we did not know how it feels not to succeed, how would we value success?

Success is not the absence of failure; it is the power to conquer failure. There is no life without the possibility or actuality of failure.

Preventing or recovering from failure will motivate you to succeed. Failure is what defines your success.

You cannot get up unless you fall. You cannot succeed unless you fail. When a child starts walking or speaking, it falls and stumbles. You will never see a child speaking clear sentences or walking smoothly from the very beginning. It is just not technically possible. Similarly, you cannot succeed without failing.

Failure is the first attempt in learning, but given the facts, can you learn from your failures? A person cannot succeed if he or she lives with failure. Failure and success cannot reside in the same body. Failure and success cannot live on the same street.

Many people do not realize that we must let go of failure. Our failures are in the past. It is said that when you are looking back, you cannot move forward. We must let go of our past failures before entering new beginnings. We cannot cling to our past and enjoy our future at the same time.

> *You cannot get up unless you fall. You cannot succeed unless you fail.*

You cannot grab hold of the bright future of successes while holding on to the dark past of failures. This is not emphasized enough. Failures come to teach us, not to leave scars. If we do not let go of our failures, we will remain dysfunctional and even damaged. We should use our failures as a pulley that helps to lift us, not a rubber band that drags us backward.

God does not want us to sulk in our failures for eternity. Our failures and the failures of others teach us to avoid repeating the same mistakes. If we touch a hot kettle once and burn our fingers, we will learn not to touch it again. The first person to touch a hot kettle and get burned teaches others not to get burned. Failures can teach us. They can teach us what to do and what not to do.

> *Our failures and the failures of others teach us to avoid repeating the same mistakes.*

People who understand the reason they fail properly examine their situation and do not fail twice. Even if they fail again, they assess and analyze their situation and don't repeat the same mistake thrice. This is how we get better. This is how we succeed.

When I was young, my mom bought the cleaning solution, Formula 409®. One day I was contemplating the reason behind such a strange name. My mom saw my puzzled face and asked, "do you know why it is called 409?" I replied "no."

Then she told me that the people who came up with the formula tried 408 times to get the formula right before succeeding in the final 409th attempt.

It took them more than four hundred times to achieve the desired result. Imagine if they would have given up on the 408th attempt. Would they have developed the effective formula they have today? This is how peculiar success can be.

You never know how near or far you are from being successful. Therefore, you should keep on trying and improving. Practice makes improvement. You fail when you think you have failed. Do not let anyone convince you otherwise. Do not give your strings to someone else to control. When you become someone else's puppet, and let them control you, you fail.

Do not let someone else's words or actions determine your actions. You decide for yourself what to do and what to say. do not let others convince you of something that is not applicable to your future. You alone are responsible for your destiny.

People will throw stones at you, but you decide whether you will turn those stones into steppingstones, or stones that break you. Ask yourself what kind of paradox of a life you are living in. If you believe what the toxic and negative people say more than what you believe, who has the power over you?

If you allow the action of others to make you angry, confused, resentful, or bitter, you no longer have control of your life. That is a failure at the base because you have allowed somebody to control you.

> *You fail when you think you've failed. Do not let anyone convince you otherwise.*

Embrace failure and embrace where you came from. Embrace those days when you were downtrodden and hurt; when you felt wronged and failed because those are the days that made you believe in the opposite of what you were feeling. If you do not embrace those, you will never reach your dream. A dream without work is a nightmare.

Many live in a nightmare because they refuse to work for their dream. Many procrastinate, become resentful, and start to feel like a failure. They feel as if time is passing by faster than it should. These are the things that make many people eternally unhappy.

Yesterday is prepared by what you have learned from it. However, if you are emotionally burdened by, and attached to the pain that you keep repeating and playing over and over in your head, you will always be a failure.

Thinking that you are too old, you're too young, you're too black, you're too white, you're too fat, you're too brown is self-defeating. All of those are labels, and when you live a label, you will never get to success. You will stay a failure. The more you know, the more you grow. When you understand this, that's the beginning of life.

## CHAPTER 4

# G in Greatness is for YOU

*Patience is not the ability to wait, but the ability to keep a good attitude while waiting.*
*— Anonymous*

Change is a gradual process. Many find the process irritating because they want immediate gratification or immediate change. Like instant coffee, instant oatmeal, instant noodles, they want things to happen instantly. They want a feeling of being full or being content instantly. However, greatness is developed over time. It is never a quick fix for a minute problem.

Ponder over your problems and try to reach the core. Try to reach the cause, rather than blaming the symptoms. We can never solve an internal problem immediately because what people do not see is what is inside of us called greatness. That is the emotional connection. We are emotional beings, and emotion is the center of our thinking and acting.

We are so used to seeing the actions of others that we do not see the emotion behind them. When we judge people by their action and miss the emotion, this is called a "miss in communicating."

When there is a miscommunication in any relationship, there will be destruction. There will be a destructive feeling, and when the relationship passes, destruction leads to dislocation. Because we are dislocated, we start looking for tanks to fill that emptiness in our life and that is where the "G" comes in. The "G" in greatness is the good that God has put in you. Man cannot measure that.

When we measure our success with each other, there is always going to be a failure because success and failure are measured by what you compare yourself to.

As I said, I did not know I was poor until I came to the United States and saw poverty. I did not know I was weak until I saw somebody who was weaker than I was. When I stopped measuring myself to other people, I realized how fortunate I was.

People should never be your measuring stick. You may not preach like Peter, but you can always help like Paul meaning be the best version of you.

When I started measuring myself according to people's standard, I missed the greatness in myself because I started looking at their standard of life. That is why one person's standard is not yours, because you cannot change something you didn't create.

Remember the whole part of life. You cannot change something you did not create no matter how hard you try. We only end up having a tough time, and knocking our heads against the wall. That knocking will never change the wall or affect it, but it will certainly damage you.

When you understand what is inside of you, you can open the door and walk through it. You will not look for external satisfaction. This action must arise from a direction that comes from the essence of who you are.

*When you live somebody else's dream, that dream becomes your nightmare.*

There is resilience in that greatness no matter how far we fall, how long we fail, or how impoverished we become. If there is a glimmer of that greatness inside you, you will prevail.

In society, we have failed to understand this because we look at what people do. Then, we start trying to emulate them, and when you emulate somebody, you miss your greatness, then you are going to fall for the confusion of life.

> *You don't know how powerful you are until you step into your greatness.*

When you live someone else's dream, whether they are your parents, your teachers, a sibling, or society, that dream becomes your nightmare because it's a dream that was never meant to be for you.

That is why even Joseph couldn't live somebody else's dream and was thrown into a pit to realize that. When we fail, we may see that as the end of the greatness inside us, but that is when the greatness starts.

Your words create that greatness. Your words program your mind. Problems do not have a solution, but challenges do. If you re-program your mind by rethinking your words, you will start to see change in your life that will totally transform it. That greatness, the ancestor of greatness, is the power you speak because the power you speak becomes the reality that you live.

The most challenging thing for us to do is to believe in ourselves. We are our greatest critics, and our greatest enemy. The enemy is not outside. The enemy is within. If you cannot deal with and conquer the enemy within, you do not have a chance against those outside because you are the first enemy (in me) that you must conquer.

Greatness is developed by the attitude and gratitude you bring to yourself. That does not come by wishing or wanting. It comes by doing. When greatness is activated, it is like a spark that creates a fire, and that little spark can destroy a fear.

That little spark can destroy doubt. That little spark can destroy pride. A little spark can do great things for you if you know how to activate it with your words.

You do not know how powerful you are because you have not tapped into that greatness yet. You do not know how powerful you are until you step into your greatness. That greatness does not mean that you're not going to find failure. It does not mean that things will never go wrong in your life.

Unmet expectations always bring disappointment. The greater your expectation, the greater your disappointments. That is called a mismatch. A mismatch is the distance between what you have and what you want. Ironically, greatness can be found in the conflict.

Greatness does not depend on your circumstances. It does not depend on what you face. A lot of times, we do not change because we cry about the problem and wail about the situation to the wrong person. So many times, we look for somebody to solve our problems. We forget that the power has been given to us.

People often ask, "What is my purpose?" "How do I know what my calling is?" "How do I define what I'm good at?" I tell them, "Whatever irritates you is your purpose and that is what you are created to solve." What defines you is a problem that you are willing to step in and solve.

Your greatness is not for you. Like the oyster that forms a pearl around the irritant, which is single gain of sand in its shell, the inadequacy in your life becomes coated with a power of greatness to turn the problems that you face into pearls. Pearls of wisdom that you can pass on. Pearls of success which can lead other people to greatness.

Greatness cannot be defeated. Greatness cannot be changed. Greatness cannot be divided. Greatness can only be enhanced. You can take two actions with greatness. You can either accept greatness or reject it.

**CHAPTER 5**

# Hope Without A Plan Is Failure—Work Your Plan

*By failing to prepare, you are preparing to fail." — Benjamin Franklin*

Hope is a dangerous thing if unaccompanied by action to support the cause. Did you open the door to success? Have you invited blessings and plentiful bounties in with your mindset, your actions, and your thinking?

Many people hope to be successful. Many people hope for a good relationship. All of us hope to be healthy, but hope without a plan will leave you hopeless. We must make every use of our manual. You must work your plan, and when you work your plan, you are moving in faith. Hope is the center of love and faith.

We all hope for something, but we do not always put a plan into action. There is a talented actress who has won Academy and Grammy Awards. She was giving an interview at 77 years of age. As she remembered her childhood, and how her family mistreated her, she started crying and sobbing like it had just happened yesterday.

That is when I came up with the concept of hope without a plan will leave you hopeless to heal. She did not have a plan to heal after all those years since her childhood trauma, so she stayed hopeless.

*Whatever you practice in life, you will become.*

As a result, she remained stuck and glued to her emotional damage because she had no plan of action to get out of the failure that she experienced. For this reason, failure should be viewed as a new beginning.

When you start a new beginning, you are no longer controlled by the past. We all have a past, but our past becomes our future when we do not let it go.

Many people begin to feel destitute when they hope and pray for something with all their might, but it does not happen the way that they want it to happen. What should they do when they have fasted and prayed? The answer is persistence. Many give up too quickly.

Bad habits die hard. If we have a habit of procrastination, a habit of lying, a habit of stealing, and we seek redemption of our deeds, we must be persistent about changing those habits if we want things to turn out differently.

For instance, if you have been eating unhealthy and not exercising for years, and now are more health-conscious and start changing those unhealthy habits, you cannot expect to be healthy in a week. You must be persistent and stick to the new healthy plan, and soon you will see results. You can't expect to immediately unravel something that has taken you years to become entangled in.

> *Invite blessings and plentiful bounties in with your mindset, your actions, and your thinking.*

What do you want? What are you believing for? When you persist in what you want, it becomes a reality to you. When you persist in love, hate leaves. When you persist in wealth, poverty leaves. If you do not persist in what you want, you're going to resist the very thing that you need. The only thing that matters is the effort we put in. So please think of the wealth and value of your goal when you strive for it.

Is your goal too weak, too meek, and too invaluable that you decide you give up after a few tries? We live in a microwave and instant society. We have instant oatmeal, instant coffee, microwave meals and unfortunately, we have become an instant generation.

In reality, things do not come to us instantly. If you do not persist in what you believe, you're going to resist the very thing that you need. It is the persistence that reduces the resistance.

I once had a male client who came in for a session. He said, "I have seen no change in my life. I've been coming to you for five months and there has been no change." I asked him, "How old are you, Sir?"

He said, "50 years of age." I replied, "Give it 50 years. You cannot be doing wrong so long and become strong in that wrong to see instant changes, but when he put the work into practice, he will see the changes."

You cannot always expect to see substantial changes in only four to five months of working toward changing something you have been doing for 50 years. This is not fruit cleanliness. Washing fruit does not affect the root.

Some people have suppressed their feelings for many years, and the root trauma is deep down.

This man's problem was not drug addiction. A family member had abused him as a child. As an adult, he struggled to be around his abuser at family functions. He did not know what to do with his feelings, so he used drugs, alcohol, and other addictions to cover his pain. Addiction only puts a temporary band-aid on the symptoms.

Some people get so desperate and destitute that they become dependent upon something to succeed, but they do not work for it.

You must work your plan. You cannot be thirsty and sit down with the hope that God will give the water to you. He gave you a brain. He gave you limbs that work. The rest depends upon the grit you hold.

There is no magic to it like Jack and the Beanstalk with his magic beans. This is something that you must work on. This is not something that you plant, and then the next day there is a big tree with fruit on it and something that leads you to a treasure.

As children, we were taught magic beans helped Jack. The fairy godmother helped Cinderella. Prince Charming will help you. Is there a magic potion? No!

I tell the people who come to me right up front, "I do not have a magic wand. I don't have a special potion because if I had a magic wand, I would use it on myself first. If I had such a potion, I would want to drink it first."

People often ask the question, "Why do bad things happen to good people?" Truth is, we are not good people. Yes, some of us do some good things and because we do some good things, we call ourselves good people.

*If you don't persist in what you want, you're going to resist the very thing that you need.*

The truth is! If you want to know how bad we are, try not giving a good person what he or she wants, then you will see how good he or she really is.

You don't have to stay wrong. You don't have to stay wicked. You don't have to stay mean, nor do you have to stay destitute because of the salvation that is freely given through faith in Christ. You don't have to pay for it, but with human beings, you must pay for what you get.

I tell people what I do is very simple, but if I give it to you without a cost, you will disrespect it; because whatever a man gets for free, he will devalue it. The question they should ask is, why do good things happen to bad people?

Failure is something that brings out the worst in people, the worst being desperation, vice, evil, and hatred. Therefore, work towards your plan or see it forever as a failure.

**CHAPTER 6**

# A Man Without A Manual Is A Mule

*In civilized life, law floats in a sea of ethics.*
*— Anonymous*

Having a manual is essential. However, that does not mean people should not live spontaneously and in the moment but in the practice of their lives.

Every product that comes on the market has a manual. A manual tells you how something works. If something malfunctions in your life and you want to know what went wrong, go to the manual.

The manual will tell you to be patient. It'll tell you to be kind. It tells you to do all those things. The manual will tell you when you get impatient. The manual tells us how to have peace no matter what storm we might face.

The manual tells us how grace empowers us. If we live by the peace and grace, if we live by the power of God inside of us, it frees us from relying on the law or man-made instructions.

# Hope Without A Plan Is Failure

I had dealt with a lot of teenagers who say they are smart, intelligent, and beautiful. When they get into a conflict and become upset because someone called them stupid, a coward or some other name.

> *If someone can cause you to be angry, hurt, or resentful, you're no longer in control of your life.*

In response to their statement, I would say, "I'm confused. You told me that you are smart, intelligent, and beautiful; and you are all those things, but why are you believing what someone else says about you to become more important than what you can do or is known as true about yourself."

Many people who have adopted this concept. Emotion really yokes them and they make someone else's lie bigger than their truth. This is precisely why humans need a manual. A manual helps us find a piece that we cannot find in a human relationship. A manual helps us find a power that we have been disconnected from possessing.

What if you build an airplane and forget to put the screws in place? You will have a beautiful airplane, but when you fly that airplane, it will certainly fall apart because you missed the essential things: the screws. That is what a manual is.

The manual gives you the essential steps to put things into practice before you allow somebody to irritate you because practice makes improvement.

If someone can cause you to be angry, hurt, or resentful, you are no longer in control of your life. That is why a manual holds significant importance. It will give you the power to hold on. It will help you not to feel powerless.

## Hope Without A Plan Is Failure

They will give you the energy, so you do not feel so defeated. It will give you the fortitude to stand firm, even when everybody else said that you would never be anything in this life.

My life, in the beginning, was no walk in the park, but one thing I did not do was give up on the greatness inside me. I did not give up on the hope I had inside of myself because that was the hope given to me by the manual.

I still read the manual. I believe the manual. I try my best to live by the manual. When you live by the manual, you will understand the need for a manual because of what you do, you will become. That is why the manual is essential. It gives you the tools that you have neglected to use.

Do you know what I tell people when they come to me? I say that this is an apprenticeship. You came to me with an empty bag, with no tools in it. Sometimes people only have one tool, a hammer. You cannot use a hammer for everything. What if you need to put up a mirror or something delicate, you cannot use a hammer? But if you use a mallet? You can put up the delicate stuff.

That is what I do. I give you the tools you need in your tool bag. When you leave here your bag will be filled with what you need so you will be able to distinguish right and wrong. The Agency is called CAYA: Come As You Are in the natural, but in the spiritual CAYA means Christ Always Your Answer.

Darkness can never overcome the light. The manual exposes the darkness in our life. Abuse is darkness. Poverty is darkness. Fear is darkness. Insecurity is darkness. When you have the manual, it gives you the opposite. Instead of being sick, you are cured. You are empowered. Instead of being afraid, you are enlightened. Instead of being abused, you now are shining like a star.

The only reason somebody can hurt you, whether it is your father, mother, friend, or enemy, is when they are emotionally dead. What they meant for evil the manual now will give you the power to turn it around to become your good. You do not have to dwell on the past. You don't have to stay yoked to it.

Abused people stay yoked when they have no relief. Some begin to hurt others as they have been hurt. They start doing the very thing that they hate. This resembles an animal more than a person. Open your manual because a man without a manual is a mule, and you know what a mule does? It moves without direction or intention. It does this without reasons or emotions, just actions. Hold fast to your foundation and build a solid manual to become a person who has their views clear.

## CHAPTER 7

Who Changed Your Story From Glory?

*Our greatest glory is not in never falling, but in rising every time we fall.*
*— Confucius.*

The glory belongs to God and your story belongs to you. The reason that your story has changed is that somebody spoke something negative and hurtful into your life. When this happens, it causes people to act from a place of weakness or bitterness. They begin to write their story from a point of pain because somebody changed their story from glory. The story is yours. That is why when you give the glory to God, He will give you the victory.

I would ask people when they come to CAYA, "who are you?" I would get a reply, "I don't know." If you do not know who you are, you will fall for anything, and you will allow someone or anything to change your story.

Somebody told you that you are abusive. Somebody told you that you are an alcoholic; that you were a drug addict. Somebody told you that you are a thief, and a liar, and then you started believing in that. That is why they could change your story because you started living that other story.

You start becoming that story and living somebody else's dream. Their dream becomes your nightmare. When you live someone else's story, it becomes your downfall. Your story is the word you spoke to yourself. Your story is the word that you build your life on.

When you were a child, you did not have a voice. This is the most challenging thing that keeps us yoked to our past. When you don't have a voice as a child, you will never develop one as an adult because you do not know who you are.

That is why when somebody asks you, who told you were a thief? Who told you that you are a liar? Who told you that you are a victim? The person who told you those things will usually be people who had the same story.

This is why there is no honor amongst thieves. They cannot trust another person. They believe that another person is going to do to them what they do to others. The hardest thing with humans is that they fall from glory.

Kids are born with the ability to face the challenges of life, but if they have been told a lie, they will live a lie. If they have been told the truth, they will live the truth.

It is all about who told them the story. The storyteller must be revealed so that you have no reason to stay stuck. The reason that you wouldn't step out, or launch into the deep, is because somebody told you that you were insecure. Somebody told you that you will always be poor. Somebody told you that you are not intelligent. Somebody told you that your skin was the wrong color. Somebody told you that you are a female and will never be anything.

*When you find your truth, you can conquer mountains.*

When you believe something, and you put work into that belief, nothing can stop you. When you have the power to go forward nothing can stop you, no matter how much you've been defeated, no matter how much you get knocked down because your story is safe. This is not the end of your story...it is the new beginning.

When you fail, you have a chance to write another story. Everybody comes to this world glorious, but somebody says something to them, and then they start to lose their glory. That's why the glory belongs to God, but the story is your victory.

When you find your story, you become victorious. When you find your story, even when you've been abused, you're not a victim anymore. When you find your voice, just because you came from poverty, you understand that you don't have to stay poor.

*When you believe something, and put work into that belief, nothing can stop you.*

When you find your truth, you can conquer mountains. A bumblebee, even for the size of its body and its wing, according to thermodynamics should not be able to fly, but it continues to fly.

Why? Because nobody changed its story, or told the bumblebee that it couldn't fly. The question I ask you today is, who told you? Who changed your story? Because if somebody had told the bumblebee, "Hey you know your body is too big for your wings. You can't fly. You will cause more damage than good. You're going to hurt yourself, and then you will not be able to do nothing in life." It would have that story, and it would have still been sitting idle right now, not being able to fly.

You're not flying in life today because you believed somebody's lie. You are not rich in life because you believe somebody else's fear. You are not healthy in life because you believe someone else's insecurity.

You are not wealthy in life because you believe somebody's limitation. They changed your story from growing, and made it into a horror story, instead of a glorious story.

You can't solve an internal problem with an external solution. The story started inside of us, and it must be changed inside of us; because again, you can be in poverty, but you don't have to be poor on the inside. That's why people from poverty can get into wealth. They didn't let poverty get inside them.

Anger is an emotion, and when it is not expressed, it can become deadly. If you don't deal with the anger inside of you, it will come outside of you and it will become violence. When we have been traumatized as children, we become traumatic or dramatic as adults.

When emotions are not handled properly you may experience many mental illnesses and mentally delayed abuse by trying to change the outside rather than the inside. We are tempted to punish the outside. We may be led to punishing the effect. The reason that some of us punish what we see is that we can't see the part that has motivated us.

The law doesn't work in this culture because it punishes the behavior and not the emotion. That's why a lot of things don't work in this society because it punishes the behavior, but not the emotion, not the essence of what we are. That's why when you punish the physical, without dealing with the internal, it becomes worse.

---
*Meekness is not weakness; it is power under control.*

---

A caterpillar endures a lot to become a butterfly, but it always behaves like a caterpillar because it doesn't know what it is now. It just believes the story somebody else has told it. We must reflect on what we are to recognize the problems and how to solve them. The point of a manual is it must be put into practice. It isn't significant until you put it into practice, just like in our life.

Hope without a plan will leave you hopeless. We all hope to be wealthy. We all hope to be better citizens. We all hope to be peaceful, but we don't have a plan of action. When you do the plan of action, your hope is your plan, but your work is the transformation around it.

The most challenging thing for us human beings is to be still when others are chaotic, being truthful when others are lying—being just when others are the picture of injustice. When you're still, you will realize what faults accompany you. You cannot see your reflection when water splashes with anger and hurt, but when you're still, the true power inside of you genuinely reveals itself.

Meekness is not weakness; it is power under control. I have the power to hurt you, but I choose not to hurt you. The power that I possess is the power that I choose. I am given the choice of love or hate. My love for you must be greater than my hate for you.

---

*Hope without a plan will leave you hopeless.*

---

Sometimes I ask people, "If this was your last moment on earth, what would you ask God for?" Most people say that they ask for more time, but time without matter is useless. Matter without space is meaningless.

We dwell in time, matter, and space. Matter is made of liquids, solids, and gases. Space is composed of length, width, and breadth.

Time is the past, present, and future. Each of these three are a trinity.

Human beings are a trinity as well. We are mind, body, and soul. We think, we feel, and we react. We are naturally inclined to misuse the privileges of the trinities. That's why we get in trouble. Therefore, the manual is essential for life's journey. We cannot function properly without the manual.

Why ask for more time if you haven't used the time that you have today? You don't need more space if you have not used the space that you already have. If you never explored the possibility of not giving into fear, why ask for more of anything until you have used up what you already have.

Others may be able to put obstacles in front of you, but you have the power to destroy those obstacles before they invade your life.

## Hope Without A Plan Is Failure

When somebody changes your story, you look outside rather than inside of yourself. Everything that you need is inside of you. It is called the seed of life.

So many people are afraid to take a leap of faith because they think it wouldn't work because Charlie Brown said it wouldn't work or because Annie Sue said it wouldn't work; however, go to the manual for yourself. Take a leap of faith and do what it says. Don't get stuck living in somebody else's story because somebody else's dream will become your nightmare.

When you live another person's dream, it becomes your ruin because it is not your truth. People living someone else's truth become confused in their own identity. It is a split in your personality. You don't know whether to believe what your eyes see or what your mind is thinking. That's what schizophrenia is all about.

The mind is powerful. Your imagination is the door to your future. The only thing that matters in life today is what you do today. If you try to think too far ahead then you will stifle your imagination. This causes both psychological and economic problems.

Most of the mental problems of today are not psychological. They are economical. The economic foundation of any culture is fundamental, and it must be collective. Poor people stay poor because they don't collectively pool their two cents together. They stay isolated.

What we need is a group mentality that is in tune with the group economy to eliminate poverty. The group mentality guides those who create laws to control judges and law enforcement. The next stage is controlling the media, who tells your story, and it goes right down to the educational system.

We have been taught that education is the key to life, but, no! Education is a tool for a fool who doesn't know any better. Financial security is actually the key to life. When you are financially secure, it doesn't matter who doesn't like you. They can't stop you from living.

---

*Remember, everything has an expiration date. If we don't use our minds, we will lose our minds!*

---

Both media and education have the power to affect our imaginations because we are social beings, we need boundaries. Imagination must have boundaries to keep us safe. This is something we should never forget.

We can see the need for boundaries as we witness the dangers of social media. Those who suffer from social media are the ones that don't know when to stop because their boundaries have been destroyed. The support that they need can never be found through social media. The two groups of people suffering the most from social media are kids and the elderly.

> *Your imagination is the door to your future.*

A major part of our human existence is learning from others. If you're the most competent person in your group, it's time to get in another group, so that you can grow and expand. If you are the most informed person in your occupation, then look for someone who knows some things that you don't so you can improve your skill level.

Remember, everything has an expiration date. If we don't use our minds, we will lose our minds! If you don't use your hand for a long time, it will get weak. We must recognize how delicate our minds are, and how it can be contaminated and useless because we allow fear, doubt, and pride to invade our minds.

The reason that a child's behavior triggers us is because it reminds us of our own past childhood traumas. Remember what a trigger is. A trigger is an unresolved childhood experience that we bring into adulthood.

For example, when someone is traumatized as a child, they become traumatic as adults. When they are triggered, there is a triggered response because the trauma that happened initially occurred inside the person, not outside of them.

They did not have a voice or choice in the matter. We are powerless as children, but powerful as adults to change the traumas of the past into the triumphants of today.

People experience hurt, depression, and depravity in diverse ways. I counseled a client who went through an awful job experience with her previous employer. She explained that her boss seemed to be a narcissist who insisted that everything was done his way.

She said that it seemed as if he thought he was the only person who mattered. She had to deal with his problems along with her own. She felt unappreciated, and he did not compensate her for the extra voice. She could not make decisions.

She later learned that her boss had been abused as a child, so he became a narcissist who found satisfaction in abusing others. He started loving himself more than others.

The word love is used loosely because many of us do not know what love is. No human being really knows what love is because love is not natural, it is supernatural. People often think of love as what we indulge or consume. But indulgence is self-seeking. Indulgence is not love, it's lust!

Lust is the desire to get something at the expense of others, while love is the desire to give at the expenses of self. Falling in love is never good because if you fall in love, you will leave the door open to fall out of love as soon as you don't get what you want.

Love can be demonstrated by what each letter symbolizing in the word LOVE. The letter "L" in love means listen. You must listen to each other. We hear with our ears, but we listen with our heart. For example, divorce and broken relationships are the results of a heart of flesh that has become a heart of stone. A Heart of stone cannot love.

The letter "O" in love means to overlook. When you love someone, you overlook their faults. We assume many things about others, which often leads to disappointment. Assumption is the lowest form of knowledge.

We all have faults. All of us are guilty of something. A guilty person will never set you free. When we recognize the guilt of our own life, will we see the favor, fortitude, and strength of another person.

The "V" in love is for value. Value is the essence of love. It's the center of love. When people don't value your heart, they do damage and hurt your heart. When people don't value your heart, they don't value your happiness.

The letter "E" is to express. Your words are expressions of your behavior. Your words have the power to condemn or to free you. Your words have the power to bring healing or hurt. Your words have the power to liberate or enslave. Your words have the power of life or death. Your words tell your story, so speak your words because it has the power to bring healing or to bring hurt.

**CHAPTER 8**

# What You Are Willing To Die For?

*You're not really ready to live unless you know what you're willing to die for.*
— *Rick Warren*

## Hope Without A Plan Is Failure

Some people get confused by the concept of dying. Hardly anyone will die for bad person since we have a lust for life. We might not know what life is about or what life is made of, but we have a deep regard for is fairness.

Fairness is something we all learn as a child and continue to value for the rest of our lives. As children may not understand many things in life due to their maturity, but they understand fairness.

I have two daughters and when I would serve them a drink, my younger daughter would look at her sister's drink and she would say her sister had more than she had. She did not know the concept of what she was doing, yet she knew fairness because it was inside her heart.

If you are not willing to die for something, you will never live for anything. Your life is the essence of who you are, but when you take the

F out of the word life, which stand for faith and favor, you are left with a lie.

That is why life is to be lived with gratitude. Gratitude of God's favor and gratitude that your life matters. Life without faith is a lie. No lie can exist forever. No lie can set you free, and no lie can become the truth. That is why we either live or die.

When our heart is hurt or mistreated, we lose our lust for life. Blood is the life of every human being. Without the blood, there is no breath. Just as we need blood for our physical hearts, our emotional hearts have needs too. Emotional, blood symbolizes our belief. Without those things, there is no life.

People who understand this concept can overcome anything. We are going to have trials, or tribulation or even temptations. We may even experience tragedies, and even be tested by society, but there is greatness in each of us.

> ## *Don't allow fear to be greater than your faith.*

When you allow that greatness to be smaller than your problems, then you have no solution. This is one of the foundational elements that I use in counseling. I tell my clients that you can never solve an internal problem with an external solution. That is how we become addictive to so many things, and addiction is a cover up for pain.

Whatever you practice, you become. If you practice drinking, you can become an alcoholic. If you practice taking drugs, you will become a drug addict. If you practice lying, you become a liar. If you practice stealing, you become a thief because what you practice, you become.

I am never surprised when someone treats me with contempt or disdain. I'm never surprised when someone tries to take my life without a reason. I'm never surprised when someone wants to hurt me and do wrong things to me because we are negative by nature (born) and pessimistic by nurture (learned).

A man without the Spirit of God is nothing but an animal, but even animals don't treat each other the way we treat each other. When an animal is full, it would not bother you. Many human beings harm one another for no good reason.

If you have ever attended the circus or a show where there are animals, and the trainer puts his head in the lion's mouth and it does not shut down on the trainer's head, it is not that the lion is dumb, but it is because the lion is full. It would not harm the trainer because it lives on instinct. Conversely, even if humans are physically full, they would still try to harm or hurt each other because they may be spiritually dead, which means that some animals would treat each other better than some humans would treat each other. Come on now!

> *Fear, insecurity, rejection, doubt, and pride are all infections that lead to death.*

We all need to avoid being that type of person. The reason we have laws is because of the absence of love. If we are not ruled by love, then we must be ruled by laws. When there is no love in a community, the law must prevail. When there is no love in a nation, the law is the only thing that holds it together.

Look within yourself. See your faults, embrace them, and try to change them. Identifying the problem is the first step in taking your life back. Whenever a doctor is treating a patient, he must first diagnose the problem. Likewise, a person must dive deep inside himself to figure out what it is that is stopping him from accomplishing the goals of being happy or being successful.

Then, when you find out the cause, you must kill it. Do not allow fear to be greater than your faith. Do not allow the past to be greater than your future. Whatever infects you will affect you.

When we discipline our children, we need to consider the infection of their behavior, not just the symptoms. The doctor that treated me for my stab wound did not know that I was bleeding internally, and the situation became chaotic.

Fear, rejection, doubt, and pride are all infections that lead to death. They are painful emotions that have physical manifestations. And the more we experience these emotions, the more they become a part of our lives, which leads to addictive behaviors.

Healing yourself is equivalent to dying to yourself, so you live again. That is the only way to live when the revelation comes, and that is the precise moment when you will be able to retrieve the gift of life to its full extent.

Are you unfulfilled, incomplete, or discontented? Then, you must retrieve the gift of life to its fullest, and then be grateful for God's benevolence upon you. Live your life to the fullest—one which you are meant to live. Don't be ungrateful for this precious gift by living a life of chaos.

Go ahead, take that leap of faith you have always wanted to do. Do something a little extra than what you normally do. Be a little kinder. Share more love! Give a little extra. I know you can do it. I have complete trust in you. So go ahead and overcome life challenges without strife because there is greatness in you to give you a new story to glory!

## CHAPTER 9

# Conclusion

*A person without a plan remains hopeless, so work your plan for change.*

Age does not make maturity, because maturity comes with accepting responsibility. I am not new to this, but only true to this. This process is not a quick fix for what we have experienced over the years because we did not get here overnight.

We have been doing wrong for so long; we become strong in our wrong. Change is a process and what you are learning in this book, you must put into practice because practice makes improvement not perfect like we have been taught from childhood.

The solution that is expressed in "Hope Without a Plan is Failure" is both life changing and practical. The practical part is using spiritual, physical, intellectual, economical, and social are the parts that makes up the whole: SPIES. Since we are triune beings, we need balance in our life. When we are out of balance, there is:

- Balance is the key to life.
- Communication is the basis of life.
- Agreement is the power of life.
- There must be balance in those areas of your life.

*Spiritually*: We are all spiritual beings equipped for life when we are born. As we grow, we are corrupted by our parents. Those who are present and those who are absent create fear, doubt, and pride in us.

*Physically*: Physically is how we fit into the world. People only see our behavior, but not what we are going through emotionally inside of us.

*Intellectually*: Intellectual is our emotions and what we are thinking of. Emotion is the center of your thinking and actions. No matter how or what you think, you must put action to it.

*Economically*: Economic is the key to many of our mental stresses. We have been taught a lie that education is the key to success. Education is a tool for a fool who does not know better. The key to success is financial security.

If you are financially secure, it does not matter who does not like you, they cannot stop you from living your best life. Even if you could walk on water, and you cannot pay your bills, it will leave you mentally stressed.

*Socially*: Socially is how we interact or relate to each other in the world, which is why social media is so prevalent. We do not want to feel like we are missing out on something happening in the world. Young children and older adults are affected mostly by social media because there is no boundary when it comes to their time.

The SPIES of life make improvements in your life, just as the 12 spies in the Bible who were sent out to spy the land. Ten of the spies came back with a report saying, "It was impossible, and two came back saying it was difficult, but possible" (see Numbers 13). If we follow the examples of the two who came back with a good report, then our lives would improve because impossibilities cannot be changed while difficulties can be changed.

If you are reading this book, then what you are going through may be difficult, but it is not impossible to change. If you are alive today: difficulty can be changed, so it is now up to you because there is greatness in you.

# About The Author

Maxwell Sears is the 7th child of 12 children. He was born and raised in the Bahamas. At 18 years of age, he moved to New York to attend Hunter College, where he earned a Bachelor of Arts in Psychology. He later attended Liberty University in Virginia, where he completed his Master of Arts in Professional Counseling. Mr. Sears has a dual degree in Biblical and Clinical Counseling as a Professional Licensed Counselor (LPC).

Mr. Sears opened Caya Counseling Services, INC in 2015. The CAYA stands for Come As You Are, and it is a Non-profit full-service counseling agency in Stockbridge GA. Based on the greatness is the gift of life from God.

Like most people, he has faced some difficult things in life, yet he has never allowed a problem to become an impossibility. Difficulty can change, but impossibility cannot be changed, no matter what you try or do, and the only impossibility in life is death itself. When a person takes faith out of life, all he or she will end up with is a LIE. So be faithful to the end.

www.ingramcontent.com/pod-product-compliance
Lightning Source LLC
Chambersburg PA
CBHW070924080526
44589CB00013B/1422